# The Gremlin

## 10 Tools to Shush that Negative Voice in Your Head!

**By Dr. Paulette Kouffman Sherman**

**Parachute Jump**
**Publishing**®
"Books that inspire you to love more"

Parachute Jump Publishing paperback edition, November 2019
Manufactured in the United States of America
Designed by Sara Blum


Sherman, Paulette Kouffman.
The Gremlin / Paulette Kouffman Sherman.

ISBN 978-0-9915405-2-5

1. Cognitive Psychology 2. Self-Help/Personal-Growth.
   I. Title

# Contents

# Introduction

I've been a psychologist for fifteen years and a life coach for nine. It's funny because one of the biggest obstacles that I see that stops people from moving ahead is something *invisible*. It isn't even real! It's that negative pesky voice that most of us have in our head, and I call it the Gremlin! The crazy thing is that the voice has been in there so long that most of us don't even recognize that it's there. We just think it is us! And we can't change what we don't acknowledge or understand. This is why I wrote this short book to help you recognize that voice and change what it says.

Hara Estroff Marano, Editor-in-Chief of *Psychology Today* magazine reports that the average person generates 25,000 to 50,000 negative thoughts per day. That is a ton of negativity you are programming in and it affects your thoughts, feelings, actions, and your body.

So, in this book you'll have the chance to become aware of your Gremlin, to understand what it is, and to challenge it so it doesn't stronghold your life, gifts, voice and freedom! This is one of the most powerful steps toward self-improvement you can take to free your true self and to express your true gifts without judgment, fear, or shame.

I've kept this book short because I realize that you are busy and it's hard to remember everything. Plus, I really believe that if you can integrate just these ten tools (or even a few) into your daily routine, your life will be much more free and positive.

I started writing a legacy of books, 'to inspire people to love more' after a bout with breast cancer in 2012. And while a book about the Gremlin may seem like the *opposite* of love, as a dating coach and therapist I've learned that once you *remove* obstacles to love , which is our natural state, it flows freely and abundantly.

We are not going to surgically remove your Gremlin. We will just learn to view him through the eyes of love and compassion, so you can stand your ground and rob him of his leverage: fear. A Gremlin can be a he or a she, so you decide if yours has a gender. But for the purposes of this book (to make it less confusing) I will use the pronoun "he" to talk about your Gremlin.

What follows are ten tools that will help you challenge your Gremlin on a daily basis.

So, happy reading!

I hope this helps.


My Best in Love,
Paulette

# What's a Gremlin?

**A** Gremlin is that negative voice in your head that stops you from being free. Sometimes it tries to keep you safe, to stop the pain of being judged, to prevent mistakes, or to ensure you live under the radar or remain invisible. It keeps you playing small. It's the voice of fear that wants you to stay in the familiar. It resists growth or change and it rarely says anything good!

The truth is that if your friends were always negative, full of fear, and constantly criticizing you, you'd probably not want to see them very often. Yet, you're harboring a Gremlin fugitive 24/7 within your head! It has great negative power over you and you haven't even said, "Boo!" to it. Well, we're going to change that.

There are different opinions about how we develop a Gremlin. Some say it's the internalized voice of a critical parent, authority figure or society. Psychoanalyst Sigmund Freud described the superego as internalized standards aimed at perfection, aiming to make a person act morally.

Sometimes your Gremlin might seem like a parent or societal judgment and other times not, but it is a repressive force rather than an encouraging voice.

Let's think for a moment about how you might handle a negative person in your life:

1. You might set boundaries

2. You might challenge them

3. You might spend time away from them and choose more loving people to associate with

4. If you had to spend time around them, you could strengthen your inner loving voice so that's the one you'd follow. You'd become your own biggest cheerleader.

Well, these ideas are some general ways you could begin to deal with your Gremlin. As you read on, you'll learn ten specific tools too.

First, I'm going to give you a series of examples about how the Gremlin regularly wreaks havoc in people's everyday lives!

Sheila was a woman in her 30's who was successful at work, had a boyfriend, friends and a family she loved. Her life was pretty good except her Gremlin never wanted her to make mistakes. So, when she bought something, like a quilt or a toaster oven, she'd spend days reconsidering whether she should keep it. Shopping was fraught with self-condemnation and she'd berate herself for any mistake.

Samuel was a successful chiropractor. He'd get a bonus at work and let his wife spend it all but he'd never let himself buy anything. His Gremlin told him spending on himself was frivolous and wasteful.

Lanny was a beautiful single woman who wanted to date but her Gremlin told her she couldn't until she lost 15 pounds! Her Gremlin said no man would like her being overweight. It also told her NY men only liked women in careers who were making over $70,000 per year.

Roberta wanted to be an author. She'd written many manuscripts and articles but her Gremlin constantly told her she was crazy to send her books to a publisher because no one would be interested. Her Gremlin stopped her from reaching for her dream.

Kira did well at work and her boss loved her. But her Gremlin constantly told her that she was going to screw up and look stupid. It scared her and stopped her from sharing her ideas, taking risks, or being confident of her many skills.

Tanya had a new leadership position at work. She was doing a terrific job but worried about being a leader, calling the shots, and being liked. Her Gremlin told her that being loved was more important than doing her job well. This kept her up at night and crying in the bathroom at work sometimes.

Scott was single and wanted to meet someone special. He tried online dating but also wanted to increase his confidence and ask women out in person; in bars, or other social situations. Every time he was drawn to a woman his Gremlin would barrage him with insults that deflated his confidence or made him think he'd be rejected so he'd back down.

Svetlana came from a large family that avoided feelings and communication. When she wanted to make a request of her mom about something important her Gremlin would chime in that she must not speak up because this was rude and her mom couldn't handle it. Svetlana could speak up at work and with friends but not in her family relationships.

These are just some real-life examples of how the Gremlin ruins our lives and stops us through fear tactics.

As a therapist, one of my jobs is to catch the Gremlin in action, put that sabotaging voice on loud-speaker so it can be heard, and help my client to challenge it so they can become their own best advocate and change in the ways they desire that serves them best.

When I work with these clients the first thing I point out is that the Gremlin isn't them! It's a negative voice (often not their own) that's trying to stop them from doing what is best for them. Once they realize this, they have a fighting chance to challenge it.

Next, I teach clients the ten tools and strategies to challenge their Gremlin, which you too will learn in the following chapters.

I suggest to my clients that they journal on a daily basis to implement these tools in their daily lives. So, I'm suggesting you get a journal and do this too. Every time you hear your Gremlin's voice, jot down the date, situation, and the tool you used. If you do this regularly,  eventually you may not even need your journal anymore because you'll internalize the process. Then you can challenge your Gremlin anytime, anywhere. So, read on . . .

# TOOL 1

## Challenging Your Gremlin Through Active Imagination

Okay, have you ever heard of active imagination? Psychoanalyst Carl Jung described active imagination as a meditation technique where the contents of your unconscious are translated into images and separate entities. He said it led to wholeness and could be done by visualization or automatic writing.

We are going to write a dialogue of an imaginary conversation with your Gremlin. It's important to develop a dialogue with your Gremlin so he doesn't just have a monologue!

Here's what I suggest: Label the Gremlin 'G' for short and label you as 'AS'; short for Adult Self. Let's take a situation where your Gremlin would normally pipe in, put him on loud-speaker and challenge him.

When you do challenge your Gremlin, try and defend what's in your best interest. Here are a few general tips:

**1.** Find exceptions to what the Gremlin says

**2.** Think of what you'd say back to a friend who was excessively negative

**3.** Remember your strengths

**4.** Remember what serves your growth and best interest

**5.** Ask if you are following love or fear

Okay, I like real life examples because they will help you grasp similar scenarios in your own life:

## Situation 1

Marissa is invited to be a guest on a television show to speak about her book. Her Gremlin is being very negative. She begins this dialogue:

**G:** What do you know about TV Marissa? You are going to make a fool of yourself! Maybe you should take a class first or you'll ruin your reputation!

**AS:** The only way to learn is to try things. This is a great opportunity and you're trying to ruin it for me but I won't let you. And, what reputation *would* I ruin? Right now I haven't taken risks and if I continue to live under the radar I'll never *have* a reputation!

## Situation 2

Teresa wanted to publish a book. Here is her dialogue with her Gremlin:

**G:** How can you write a book? Maybe no one will like it and you'll get bad reviews.

**AS:** That's always a possibility but I can still choose to share my gifts and express my true voice. People may dislike what I say or love it. I can't control that. I can only do my part. If I am too affected by judgment, that could keep me from sharing my message and we can't allow that!

## Situation 3

Mark wants to date but his Gremlin is messing with his confidence. Here's his dialogue:

**G:** So you want to ask a girl out! What makes you think that she'll say yes? You've been rejected before and you'll probably make a fool of yourself. What if she thinks you're a stalker?

**AS:** I may get rejected but I can't hide all my life! Many men ask women out so why can't I? As long as I don't reject myself in the process I can be proud of myself for trying. As long as I try it's a step forward; whether she says yes or no—that's on her!

## Situation 4

Galia got a lot of pressure from her family about getting married. Here's her dialogue with her Gremlin:

**G:** You are going home soon and your mom is going to be worried again that you're single. You're upsetting her. You are going to be such a disappointment.

**AS:** I can't control the fact that I haven't met someone I like, or live up to my mom's expectations. This is my life and I need to accept and love myself now. She lived her life and this life is mine to make my own choices.

Sometimes you will need to have a longer dialogue with your Gremlin to come to a conclusion. If you need to, just keep going. Here's an example of a slightly longer one:

## Situation 5

A woman named Rachel has a panic attack when she thinks a guy at work will ask her out. This is her dialogue with her Gremlin:

**G:** A male co-worker just smiled at you! He's going to ask you out! Then what will you do? You are going to get anxious and vomit at work. Then everyone will be talking about you . . .

**AS:** Whoa! I really don't want to be asked out at work. Is that going to happen? Oh God, my heart is pounding!

**G:** It should be! Usually at work you don't have to worry about dating but now you do!

**AS:** I hope you're wrong. I'm supposed to be challenging you . . . different co-workers smile at me. Maybe that's all it was and this is just a story. Maybe he won't ask me out.

**G:** Ah, but what if he *does*! What would you do? How will you work then?

**AS:** If he asks me out I can just say no! But the likelihood is that he was just being friendly. Stop caring about things that probably won't happen! I'm getting back to reality in the present, and to work!

Please take your journal, write the date, the situation, and do this type of dialogue for any challenging situation where your Gremlin pops up. Did you take control? Did you challenge him? Did this tool help you move forward in a healthy, more productive way?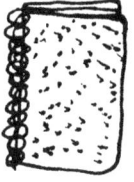

There's a Native American story about a little boy and his grandfather. His grandfather told the little boy that he had a wolf on each shoulder. One wolf was love and the other one was fear. The little boy asked which wolf would win. The grandfather replied, "Whichever one you feed the most." Which are you feeding: love or fear?

The more that you consciously practice choosing love in every moment, the more your life will expand. I have seen this help people live their dreams and have big breakthroughs. Just begin this dialogue so your true self becomes clearer, louder and more convincing than your Gremlin!

Once you journal for a while you'll notice whether there are any patterns or themes to your issues or situations. What themes do you especially struggle with? Is it judgment, appearance, perfectionism, control, being different? Understanding your theme can allow you to catch it and work with it right away. This is the hole you fall into. Try to free yourself from its power by practicing this dialogue process on a regular basis.

# TOOL 2

## Being Present: Using the Distinction of Past, Present, or Future

Here's an interesting point: The Gremlin is in his heyday when you are in the past or future. He has much less power over you when you are in the *present*!

So, this is a good way to fight that negative voice. Remember to use the distinction I'm going to give you. When you're presented with an internal or external challenge, ask yourself, **"Is this in the past, present, or future?"**

If it's in the past, there's nothing you can do about it now, so don't waste your energy.

If it's in the future, it's non-reality. It hasn't happened and may not, so why are you treating it like it's real? Tell yourself (and your Gremlin) to snap out of it!

If it's in the present moment it's real, so then you can look at it.

In my experience, less than 10% of challenging situations are in the present (when your Gremlin is chiming in) so this distinction should help you a lot!

Although it's a simple tool it can be tricky to decipher, so let's practice with this distinction in a little quiz here. Circle whether the situation is a past/present/future scenario:

**1.** Your Gremlin says you won't be picked for the softball team at work in June.

Past / Present / Future

**2.** Your Gremlin says the reviewers will hate your new book.

Past / Present / Future

**3.** Your Gremlin says that all men will leave you, just like your last boyfriend did.

Past / Present / Future

**4.** Your Gremlin says that you might make the wrong decision on your purchase of a couch and that you can't trust yourself.

Past / Present / Future

**5.** Your Gremlin says if you cut your hair no men will be attracted to you.

Past / Present / Future

**6.** Your Gremlin says that you will get sick again, after a bout with cancer.

Past / Present / Future

**7.** Your Gremlin says that your family didn't think that you were smart so your boss won't either!

Past / Present / Future

Some of these examples are *both* past and future or present and future but none are truly just in the present. Do you get it?

From now on, I always want you to notice your Gremlin and even before you examine the *content* of what he's saying, just ask, "Is this in the past, present or future?" And if it's in the past or future say, "I can only deal with what is now. "

If you follow this prescription you will stop your Gremlin in his tracks and gain amazing power back without unnecessarily draining your energy. Write this distinction on a notecard and carry it in your wallet. It's better than money.

Let's try a few examples before moving on to the next tool. (We will do this in dialogue format again, G for Gremlin, AS for adult Self).

## Example 1

**G:** You'd better change jobs soon because I read that people make the most progress in their career before they are 40 and you're 37!

**AS:** You are talking about my future. I'm not 40 yet and I don't want to change jobs right now so this is not reality. Thanks for sharing.

## Example 2

**G:** You aren't making enough money. What if you can't pay the mortgage in a year and you have to sell your house and move to a bad neighborhood with your kids, or worse, move in with your parents!

**AS:** You are talking about the future. I am paying the mortgage and am living in a good neighborhood. Stop trying to scare me.

# Example 3

**G:** Your last two boyfriends broke up with you and one cheated. Sure, things seem to be going well with Ron for a year now but what if the same thing happens with him?

**AS:** This is a fear about the future, which is not present reality. I am focusing on now and I am *happy* now!

For homework I'd like you to use this PAST/ PRESENT/FUTURE distinction in your daily life, journal the outcome and whether it helps.

# TOOL 3

## The Angel On Your Shoulder: What You Focus on Expands

Just like the Native American story about the two wolves, you always have a choice about whether to focus on fear or love. What do you choose in each moment?

We've talked a lot about the Gremlin but what about your angel or Higher Self? This voice always wants your highest good and comes from a place of love so it's important to develop a relationship with it too and to feed *this* voice.

You can do an active imagination dialogue with your Higher Self too and get to know this voice better and begin to listen to it instead of your Gremlin.

Take some deep breaths, close your eyes and imagine a fairy light inside your soul that only knows love, growth and your highest good. It is wise and views things from an expanded perspective. It's easier to connect to this voice when you're in a state of relaxation and receptivity, so you may want to practice deeply breathing for ten minutes first. This is your love consciousness. In contrast, your Gremlin takes center stage when you are panicked, stressed, or in a fear-based state.

In his book, *Power Versus Force*, Dr. David Hawkins discusses how emotions have different frequencies or levels of consciousness. He created a "Map of Consciousness" through kinesiology testing, and his map represents logarithmic calibrations of levels of human consciousness from 1-1000. The significance in his scale lies not in the number itself but in the relationship of one number to another. It shows how our consciousness rises as the frequency (numbers) ascends.

I want you to understand his map of consciousness so you will see that your feeling states have a certain vibration, and that the frequency rises as the emotion you vibrate becomes more positive and loving. I will briefly describe Dr. Hawkins Map of Consciousness so that you can see the progression of emotions:

SHAME (20) When you're in a state of shame you feel humiliated and don't feel that you're loveable.

GUILT (30) You have an unforgiving emotional attitude.

APATHY (50) You feel hopeless about life and are in a frame of mind where you no longer care what happens.

GRIEF (75) You're in a state of pain based on regret from the past. People at this level often feel depressed, and past loss colors your future.

FEAR (100) You feel anxiety and fear danger, sometimes obsessively.

DESIRE (125) Here you have a craving to expend effort to achieve goals or to gain rewards.

ANGER (150) You sometimes feel hate, aggression, and maybe even vengeance. This stems from a frustrated want.

PRIDE (175) In this state of mind we like ourselves but it's dependent upon outside things, like being a certain way and having a particular status, power, money etcetera.

COURAGE (200) Here there's a willingness to try new things and to explore with determination.

NEUTRALITY (250) Here a person isn't driven to prove anything. It's a safe level because people feel confident that they can live in the world, under most circumstances. (i.e. you may not be thrilled that you're single but you're okay with it).

WILLINGNESS (310) Here a person has overcome inner resistance to life and is committed to participating.

ACCEPTANCE (350) Acceptance means that you're in harmony

with things. You aren't very judgmental and don't come in with a huge agenda of expectations. Hawkins says that at this level, love is created within and can't be given or taken away. There is the acknowledgment that you are the source of your happiness.

REASON (400) At the level of reason, you use your higher mind, information and understanding and wisdom to function.

LOVE (500) Interestingly, Dr. Hawkins says that only .4% of the world population actually has this level of consciousness. He describes love as the ability to be in a state of giving and acceptance and possessing the ability to see the beauty in everyone. Here we create from the love in our own hearts, which isn't dependent on the other person being a certain way for you. You inclusively see the other person's essence.

JOY (540) This is when love becomes more unconditional. It arises in the moment and is full of compassion.

PEACE (600) This state is only experienced by one in ten-million people. It is a God-consciousness, full of peace.

It is easy to see that most people are in these lower states of consciousness because they are frequently listening to their Gremlin. Your Higher Self resides in that loving state of consciousness but it can require effort to connect there through deep breathing, meditation, stillness, or perhaps this active imagination dialogue exercise and active focus on that higher state of consciousness.

Let's explore some examples of a Higher Self voice in an active imagination dialogue. You will see how it feels and sounds different from your Gremlin. Let's use G for Gremlin and HS for Higher Self.

## Example 1

**G:** You can't go to the CBS show as a guest author. You will tank!

**HS:** Of course I can. I came into this world to share my gifts and I can do it or I would not have been given this opportunity. Think how many people I can help with my love and wisdom. I am an instrument of God and we're all here to share light. I will be *great!*

## Example 2

**G:** You are feeling lonely and unwanted and you may as well eat that Ben & Jerry's. You're unattractive anyway.

**HS:** You are never alone and you are *always* loved. You are a child of Source and God loves you unconditionally and wants you to love yourself that way. I know things don't feel easy today but eating Ben & Jerry's won't fix this. What you really want and need is love and acceptance. Are you willing to try and give that to yourself now?

# Example 3

**G:** In the past, bullies teased you in high school. And maybe now you won't make any friends in college.

**HS:** It's unfortunate you were hurt by bullies in high school but that had more to do with them than you. College is a whole new experience where most people will be more mature. If you are your true self you will attract the same to you. There is so much about you to love and you are a great friend. Those new people will be lucky to have you.

See how the voice of your Higher Self makes you smile instead of cringe? Isn't that who/what you'd like to hang out with 24/7?

We speak to ourselves in self-talk all the time. So ask yourself, are you being constructive or destructive with that voice? Begin to pay attention.

Practice this active imagination dialogue process with your Higher Self regularly in your journal to strengthen that connec-tion. It is well worth strengthening this voice, which can help you bring more love into your life in any scenario, should you connect with it. It will also have the domino effect of helping you use that Higher Self voice and unconditional love state of consciousness with others more!

# TOOL 4

## Be Willing to Drop It!

There's a story about two monks who arrived at a river. A young woman asked the younger monk for help to carry her across it. He said no, explaining he took a vow of chastity. She said, "I won't impede your vow I just need you to help me cross the river." He said no, but the older monk told her to climb on his back and they would cross together. On the other bank he put her down and she thanked him. As the monks walked on alone again, the younger one said, "You shouldn't have carried her. It's against our rules." The older monk replied, "She needed help and I put her down on the other bank. You didn't carry her at all and she is *still* on your back!"

This happens a lot. We all need to let go of what we can't change, and what is past and dead weight. As troubling situations arise, I want you to consider this. Ask yourself, "What dead weight am I still carrying? What am I willing to drop now?"

Think about what the Gremlin is saying to you and even if a part of it makes sense, can you drop it for the greater good? Can you let yourself be imperfect for the sake of being present?

For example, could you have done better in how you spoke to your husband yesterday? Or maybe your Gremlin is bugging you about an incident during your workday and now it's over, so will you drop it? In cognitive therapy they call this "thought stopping." People just say, "Stop!" when they are having repetitive automatic thoughts that lead them down a dark rabbit hole.

Let's look at some examples of this:

**1.** You forgot your father-in-laws birthday and you feel bad but now your Gremlin is tormenting you when you need your sleep.

Say, "Stop!" You can make it up to your father-in-law and buy a gift, but criticizing yourself isn't helpful, so drop it.

**2.** You applied for your dream job but they haven't called to offer you the job. You wish you said something different in your interview and you're replaying what you did say a thousand times over in your mind.

Drop it. You can't go backwards. You can only send a thank you note, including your thoughts that way. Refuse to drain your energy on things that are done.

**3.** You took your test and messed up five questions. You keep on thinking about it. Your Gremlin is saying how stupid you were not to know the answers.

Drop the Gremlin right now. You're carrying dead weight. The test is scored already. You can only do better the next time.

Got it? Which monk will you choose to be like: the old, wise one or the righteous, worried one?

For homework I want you to catch yourself throughout the week when you're carrying something that is clearly over. Resolve to notice the dead weight and to put it down. Don't pick it up again. Doesn't it feel great to travel so light? Your Gremlin will abhor this and you will finally align with the lightness of your Higher Self.

# TOOL 5

## Limiting Beliefs & How to Expand Them

The Gremlin traffics in limiting beliefs. These are beliefs that trap you from doing what you want to do or from moving ahead. In fact, the Gremlin uses limiting beliefs so much that he has already indoctrinated you into thinking that many of these limiting beliefs are *true*!

Let's take some common examples of a limiting belief:

# Example 1 of a Limiting Belief

**G:** You're 35 and single. No man wants to date a woman over 35.

**Challenge:** There may be some truth to the idea that men date younger women but this is changing. In a recent survey, 80% of men said they *will* date a woman five years older and 33% of men would make a long-term commitment to a woman who was ten years older.

So, your Gremlin will try and embed a blanket limiting belief such as, "No men want women over 40 and your job is to challenge it as above. Think of exceptions like Demi Moore, Madonna, your neighbor, or whomever. Get the idea? Here's another example:

# Example 2 of a Limiting Belief

**G:** Published authors always have agents, published articles, and a huge social media following of at least 5000.

**Challenge:** Although this is often true, there are exceptions. There are plenty of authors who self-published and then attracted publishers, who did not have an agent or a platform. It only takes one exception to overrule a limiting belief and to allow it to stop you from forging your own path.

# Example 3 of a Limiting Belief

**G:** Women who are mothers *have* to cook!

**Challenge:** Plenty of women have husbands who cook, nannies who cook, or they order in. There are definitely exceptions to this limiting belief but if it applies to most people, the Gremlin will use this to make you feel bad or abnormal. Choose to be you instead!

# Example 4 of a Limiting Belief

**G:** A man has to make more money than a woman.

**Challenge:** Today over 105,000 men are stay-at-home dads and surveys show many more men and women don't mind if the *woman* is the breadwinner. Times are changing and there are many exceptions to this limiting belief. (You can see more research on this in my book, *When Mars Women Date*).

Great, so now I want you to stalk the common limiting beliefs the Gremlin offers you and don't accept them as true. You need to research exceptions, challenge them, and don't let them box you in.

For homework, take your journal and write all the limiting beliefs that your Gremlin tells you and find an exception. This process will set you free to think for yourself, finally!

# TOOL 6

## Parenting Your Wounded Child

What would you say to your child if he or she were constantly listening to their Gremlin?

As a psychotherapist, I have found that people often speak much more harshly to themselves than they *ever* would to their children. So, I want you to recognize that there's a little boy or girl inside you that this Gremlin is scaring! It's time that you comforted that child.

When my daughter was three-year-old she hated monsters. She made us check under her bed for them and wanted her light on. Well, little did she know that when she grew up, she'd probably have a Gremlin inside her head that she would need to regularly expose to the light!

So suppose your child comes to you saying the things your Gremlin is saying to you: "I'm not good enough. No one likes me. I will be a failure," or something similar. I'm sure you'd be loving and comforting to your child, so now I want you to learn to respond that same way to *yourself*!

Let's practice with some examples, so that you can connect with that nurturing parental voice. Imagine talking to your child in those scenarios:

## Example 1

Your daughter Sheila comes to you crying, saying, "Johnny at school says that I'm skinny as a rail and no boys will like me. None of the girls in junior high like me either."

**You:** Sheila, you are beautiful, kind, funny, and a great friend. One day you'll probably be happy you're thin. You need to remember you're valuable and loveable and don't let others define you. Are you willing to work on that? Also, always remember that I love you just as you are!

(If you think it's good advice you can use it on yourself!)

## Example 2

Mara came home upset because she didn't make the soccer team after lots of hard work. She said, "I don't know why I try because I didn't make it and I may as well give up. I'm a loser and it seems so unfair! Maybe I'll *never* get what I want!"

**You:** Mara honey, I know that you're very disappointed but don't give up. Be proud of how hard you worked and keep trying. Sometimes it can take awhile to get results, and the only thing we can control is doing our best. But don't give up on your dreams! Why don't you ask the coach what you need to work on to make the team? Please don't give up on yourself when you feel rejected because rejection is going to be an ongoing part of life and you need to learn to be your own biggest supporter.

## Example 3

Your son Ben comes home upset because his teacher put him in "time out" for talking during circle time. He said, "She *hates* me mom! I'm always getting in trouble. I'm never going to school again!"

**You:** Ben, I know you had a really hard day and I'm sorry about that but avoiding school is not the solution. And just because you got put in time out doesn't mean that your teacher hates you. I put you in time out and I *love* you. I do it so you learn how to listen and have good boundaries. It sounds like you got a time out in school because you were talking. If you listen instead of talking, you probably won't get time out. Are you willing to try that?

Isn't that the nurturing, helpful voice you like much better than the Gremlin? I know this seems like a very simple exercise but again, I've found when we pretend to be speaking to our child (instead of ourselves) we have much better advice and are better able to stave off the Gremlin's negativity. So try it!

For homework, I want you to write about challenges that arise in your journal. Pretend your child (even if you don't have one) is coming to you with that negative voice and respond to them in a caring way. You can help them move from fear and shame to a supportive state of love, and help yourself in the process. This can help you internalize that loving parental voice when you most need it.

# TOOL 7

## "The Facts" Versus "The Story"

Another thing that your Gremlin loves to do is to take some event and create a whole *story* around it that hikes up your fearful feelings.

Your job is to squash that by using this tool: *Separate the facts from the story.*

You can become a detective and make sure that you're being very concrete. Let's try some examples:

**1.** You're dating someone new. He's called daily for two months and this time he missed a day. Your Gremlin says, "See, he's going to ditch you like all the others. He didn't call because he changed his mind or met someone else he likes better."

# The Story Versus the Facts

The *facts* are that this guy has been calling you daily for two months and he didn't call today.

The *story* you then created from the above facts is about *why* he isn't calling—he doesn't like you, he met someone else, etcetera. In a court of law he would be innocent till proven guilty but in Gremlin law it's the opposite. Remember, you aren't psychic so stick to *the facts*. Give the guy and yourself the benefit of the doubt until you've heard *his* story.

If you do this distinction of "The Story" versus "The Facts," you'll be less upset. When you look at the facts and see that he did not call for one day . . . no big deal. But when you tell yourself that he doesn't like you anymore, you will feel really bothered!

Why create a negative story with no real facts to support it?

Let's try another example:

**2.** You apply for a job in the career you want and you don't get it. Your Gremlin says, "You see! You aren't meant to be an actress and this is a sign from the universe for you to wake up and stop this!"

# The Story Versus Facts

The *facts* are that you've gotten parts before and now you got one rejection.

The *story* you then created from the above facts is about *why* you were rejected—you shouldn't be an actress, and the universe is trying to show you this. Take it down a notch and put your acting skills to the test. Pretend to be a lawyer who has your Gremlin on the ropes. Tell him that if you *were* going to create a story (not based on facts) that it might as well be a positive one! Perhaps it could be that you didn't get this part because a better one was waiting for you, on Broadway!

Get the idea? Here's your homework assignment: Next time you face a challenging situation, write down just the facts in your journal first. Then write the story that you are *making up* about it. Is it positive? Is it realistic? I guarantee this tool will help you slow down, stay grounded and in love instead of letting fear take over and make everything worse.

# TOOL 8

## Thoughts Lead to Feelings, Which Lead to Action

It's important to know this progression, which is why we've been examining your thought process here. First let me explain how thoughts lead to feeling which lead to actions:

### Example 1

Let's say that you're trying to lose weight and pledged to go to the gym every day. You did this successfully four times but the fifth weekday you flaked. Your thoughts about this will determine what happens next.

**Gremlin Thoughts:** "I suck! I already screwed up my diet so I may as well eat brownies from the fridge. I *knew* I wouldn't go to the gym!"

**Higher Self Thoughts:** Okay, I messed up today but I *did* go to the gym four times this week and that's four more times than usual! So, that's progress. Maybe next week I can try for five times but I need to give myself props for what I *did* do!

With the Gremlin thoughts the person goes downhill based on a thought that they suck, their feeling that they're hopeless, and the self-sabotaging behavior of devouring ice cream.

With the Higher Self (or more positive thoughts) the person thinks that there's improvement and things will continue to improve; this leads to more feelings of hopefulness and a greater likelihood that they will go to the gym five times next week.

## Example 2

A husband and wife have the day off from work. The wife is excited to spend romantic time alone with her husband but he is excited to spend some down time alone.

**Gremlin Thoughts:** "My husband doesn't love me so I am feeling crappy and undesirable. I may as well cry all day or divorce him."

**Higher Self Thoughts:** Okay, my husband is tired and he likes to refuel alone. He does love me and maybe we can spend some time together too. I can use the time to myself well and this will help me relax too. Then we can discuss what we can do together after.

You can see that the same situation has a different outcome depending on the thought, feeling, and behavior or action taken.

Now, for homework, you try it. I want you to write down any challenges and create two different thoughts about it: one destructive, and one constructive. Then notice how your thought  patterns lead you to different feelings and actions. And once you notice this, you have a choice.

This will help you to stop your Gremlin from jumping in and pulling you into a negative cycle.

# TOOL 9

## Tricks of the Trade

As we know by now, the Gremlin likes to magnify your fear to get a stranglehold over you so you can't move forward in life. He programs in fearful thoughts and tries to trap you into reacting six common ways that we will discuss here. To disarm him, you can notice these six reactions and try to stop yourself when you do them. Here they are, so you can understand them:

1.  CATASTROPHIZING: You expect disaster to strike and you magnify the problem.

2.  GLOBALIZING: You take one or two facts and make them global.

**3.** BLACK & WHITE THINKING: You see things as all good or all bad. There's no middle ground.

**4.** PERSONALIZATION: You think that everything that others say or do is about you.

**5.** OVER-GENERALIZATION: You take one piece of information and come to a general conclusion.

**6.** WHAT-IFS: You think of all the terrible things that *could* happen but probably never will!

Okay, let's give you an example of each of these six reactions, so you can choose a different way to respond.

CATASTROPHIZING: Julie did not put enough study time in for a test and she was feeling uneasy even though she always got A's. Her Gremlin said, "See you're going to fail this test or even the class!" The Gremlin was trying to make her believe disaster would strike.

Instead of thinking the worst, Julie can tell herself that she always does well and knows her subject. She can stay present to use the time she has left to study and she can also realize that if she got A's on two other tests that even if she got a C on this one, she would not fail the class.

GLOBALIZING: Marlene was dating a guy who put up an Instagram picture of himself with four co-workers, one of whom was a very attractive woman his age. Marlene immediately assumed since they were hanging out smiling, that they were dating. Marlene jumped to the conclusion that all men would like to date this attractive co-worker so therefore her date would too..

BLACK & WHITE THINKING: Bernard had a fight with his wife. She told him that she didn't want to speak to him when he was angry. He took this as a rejection and a sign that she didn't care about him or his feelings. He thought that if she cared about him she would talk to him immediately and fix things! To him this was the *right* approach and the situation was black and white.

Bernard's wife felt they could resolve things better once he calmed down. This was her perspective. It wasn't that she didn't care.

Relationships (and life) have shades of gray and Bernard needed to consider different perspectives and to find a middle path.

PERSONALIZATION: Tanya was a bit insecure when her husband Rick would socialize at parties and would not stay with her. She interpreted his behavior to mean that he didn't love her and that she wasn't important to him. She personalized his tendency to like group socializing when it had nothing to do with his feelings for her.

Tanya needed to remind herself that not everything is about her and that her husband just approached things differently.

OVERGENERALIZING: Millie got rejected by five guys on an online dating site. Her Gremlin said, "See, all guys online don't like you because you're 28!" She went from not hearing from five men to deciding that no men would ever contact her. This is not true and won't serve her because it only takes one to change her life!

She needs to be careful not to make her situation worse by exaggerating things in this way.

WHAT-IFS: Roberta often let her mind spin in directions that were negative and think about things that may never happen. Her kids were going swimming with their grandma. Instead of thinking about them having a wonderful time she'd think, "What if they drown?" and fill herself with fear. If she had to go to a party, instead of thinking, "What fun!" she'd think, "What if no one there talks to me?" She would imagine the most negative 'what-if' situation and kill the mood before anything started, for no reason.

She needed to stop herself and remain present.

I've given you six examples of common reactions or cognitive distortions and how you can work with them. These are the tricks of the trade for your Gremlin. If you begin having reasonable reactions, what will he do? Maybe he'll take a vacation.

This is your homework for this week: try and journal about which of these six reactions or cognitive distortions you use most and how you can react differently. Seeing yourself in action in your daily life will help you be much more aware.

# TOOL 10

## Positive Self-Talk & Affirmations

I mentioned that I'm writing a legacy of books to help people *love more*, and this book is number twenty in that legacy. So, it seems fitting not just to help you derail your inner Gremlin but to also promote improving your self-talk to affirm your self-worth and your ability to love yourself and others more.

Of course, your Gremlin hates all this positivity because it makes him uncomfortable and he becomes utterly useless in this environment. He knows he is not coming to any love-fest!

So, let's begin. For some reason we find it natural to constantly judge and criticize ourselves 24/7, but when we begin to consistently say positive things to ourselves we blush, roll our eyes, feel conceited, or think it sounds cheesy to compliment ourselves. My clients cringe if I suggest practicing affirmations in the mirror. This reminds them of that "Saturday Night Live" episode of Stuart Smalley saying, "Because I'm good enough, smart enough, and doggone it, people like me!" If you want to laugh, check it out on YouTube here: https://www.youtube.com/watch?v=-DIETlxquzY.

But, why isn't it just as unnatural to walk around saying, "I'm not special, I'm stupid and no one likes me!" They should have done an episode on that. Our self-talk and affirmations brainwash us 24/7 so we don't want to decrease the negative things that we say, we want to increase the positive.

By the way, there is research to back up the positive effects of positive self-talk and the negative effects of negative self-talk. Sports psychologists studied the benefits of positive self-talk and the deleterious effects of negative self-talk (Gould, Hodge, Peterson, & Giannini, 1989; Mahoney & Avener, 1977). Proponents of positive self-talk have suggested that positive self-talk can reduce anxiety, increase effort, and enhance self-confidence (Finn, 1985; Weinberg, 1988). A Harvard professor, Dr. Robert Rosenthal, collected the results of over 300 studies showing the Self-Fulfilling Prophecy in action. In classroom experiments, a group of children were divided into two classes. One class was given to a teacher who was told that the students were high achievers and should do well. The other teacher was told that her class was composed of underachievers who needed special help. At the beginning of the school year there was no difference between the two groups of children in terms of ability. By the end of the school year the class that was labeled 'high-achievers' was doing better than average work. The class that had been labeled as 'underachievers' was doing below-average work. Children who made gains in the 'high achiever' group were generally better liked by their teacher, but the children who made gains in the 'underachiever' class were generally less liked by their teacher! Imagine the expectations of your Gremlin for you. Do you want to meet them? No!

Your self-talk and your expectations about yourself are important! We are just looking for a few simple tools you can use in your busy day to increase your positive self-talk and expectations, today. One good way to begin this, I like to call "Flip the Switch." The way it works is to make note of the negative things the Gremlin most often tells you and to flip them proactively to *opposite* statements and write those down as affirmations. Let me give you some examples.

## Example 1

If your *Gremlin* often says, "You are going to run out of money to take care of yourself and your family."

*Flip the switch* and write, "I am abundant, successful, and effortlessly support my family's needs."

## Example 2

If your *Gremlin* often says, "The women around you are much thinner. You look tired and need to lose weight."

*Flip the switch* and write, "'I am radiantly healthy, beautiful, vital, and I love my body and myself."

# Example 3

If your *Gremlin* often says, "You will never achieve your dreams."

*Flip the switch* and write, "I am successful beyond my wildest dreams and I'm feeling infinitely blessed to be doing my soul's purpose."

Get the idea?

Some of you may not believe (per The Law of Attraction) that thinking and feeling positive things will actually bring them to you. But, isn't it better to say positive things to yourself than negative things anyway? We know your thoughts affect your feelings and actions. The Law of Attraction proponents go further to say that you vibrate (like a magnet) what you think, feel, and do, and that draws you to manifest that vibration in the outer world. Just something to consider as possible that would be a nice bonus to how good all the positive self- talk is going to make you feel!

In any event, we are proactively programming your mind to speak to you as a cheerleader or an unconditionally loving voice, and your Gremlin won't survive if you believe the opposite of some of his best attacks.

So, homework #1 in this section is to notice key attacking statements your Gremlin makes and to flip them to the opposite (as demonstrated in the above examples) and to write out the positive affirmations that apply instead. Then you can record yourself (on voice notes on your iPhone or on a digital recorder) saying these positive statements in your own voice. Then you can listen to it while commuting on a train (not driving) or when going to sleep. Do this a few times a day and it will allow these positive messages to sink in!

Here's another idea for homework #2, which is even more comprehensive. It can be helpful to consider the major life areas and think about what you'd like to happen in them and write a few affirmations for each area. For example, look at finances, career, friends, romantic life, self-care, fun, personal development, healthy, family and others if you wish. I just listed ten categories here so let's start with those. I challenge you to write five affirmations for each category or 50 in total! Think about how you will be flooding your mind, heart and even the cells in your body with love and positive self-talk! This can become a positive habit.

I am going to give you an example for each of these ten life areas so you understand how to proceed:

MONEY: "I am abundant and successful financially. All that I need flows to me."

ROMANTIC RELATIONSHIPS: "My romantic relationship is harmonious, healthy, passionate, joyful and lifelong."

FAMILY: "My family is a happy well functioning team who supports one another."

FRIENDS: "My friendships are fun, intimate, and long-lasting."

CAREER: "My career fulfills my soul's mission and I love what I do."

SPIRITUAL DEVELOPMENT: "I have a daily connection with the Divine, to my guides, and to my Higher Self."

PERSONAL DEVELOPMENT: "Every day I learn and move in the direction of my dreams and goals."

HEALTH: "I am radiantly healthy. I eat well, exercise, and relax."

FUN: "I make time for joy and play every day."

SELF-CARE: "I take impeccable care of myself."

So for homework #2 in this section, do these extended affirmations by writing them in your journal and then recording them in your voice, as described earlier. If there's a special category you'd like to add, do it!

Remember that friends may come and go but *you* are the one person you'll have for this lifetime so invest in yourself, in your energy, and in your self-esteem. You are the source of all that you do! And, the more positive you are, the more positively you affect others.

So, that is your short book to handling your Gremlin and filling your self-talk and your life with love more than fear. As short as I tried to make these chapters, it's still a lot of information and it's hard to keep it all in your head, so I'm ending this book with a cheat sheet that you can photocopy and carry around with you. It lists all 10 tools as a reminder. If you practice them in your journal, you will eventually internalize them all.

# Your 10 Tools Cheat Sheet

**1.** Challenging Your Gremlin Through
Active Imagination

**2.** Be Present: Using the Distinction
of Past, Present, or Future

**3.** Remember the Angel on Your Shoulder:
What You Focus On Expands

**4.** Be Willing to Drop It!

**5.** Limiting Beliefs & How To Expand Them

**6.** Parenting Your Wounded Child

**7.** "The Facts" Versus "The Story"

**8.** Thoughts Lead to Feelings,
Which Lead to Action

**9.** Tricks of the Trade

**10.** Positive Self-Talk
& Affirmations

# ABOUT THE AUTHOR

**Dr. Paulette Kouffman Sherman** is a Licensed Psychologist with a Master's and Doctorate degree in Clinical Psychology. She had concentrations in school psychology and family therapy. She is also a certified life coach, an author, teacher and speaker. She has worked as a healer in a variety of settings including high schools, universities, hospitals, partial programs, nursing homes, group  and private psychotherapy practices and nursery lab schools. She has worked with patients with a range of issues, including relationship issues, self-esteem, depression, anxiety, career issues, familial and personal struggles and losses. She was awarded the 'Woman of the Year' in Psychology in NY State by the National Association of Professional Women in 2013, and a 'Woman of Outstanding Leadership' in 2014 by the International Women's Leadership Association.

Dr. Sherman specializes in relationship issues and is the author of *Dating From the Inside Out: How to Use the Law of Attraction in Matters of the Heart* published by Atria Books and *When Mars Women Date*. She's the Director of My Dating School in New York City and has been a frequent speaker at The Learning Annex. Dr. Sherman writes a column as the NY Love Examiner, and has been an expert on the *CBS Early Show*, the *AM Northwest Early Show* and the *Curtis Sliwa* show on 77WABC. She has been quoted as a relationship expert in over 350 outlets such as *MSN.com*, *USA Weekend*, the *NY Post*, *Crains*, *Newsweek*, *Lifetime.com*, *More*, *Match.com*, *Foxnews.com*, *Fox Business*, *Better Homes & Gardens*, *Reader's Digest*, *Redbook*, *Glamour*, *Forbes*, *Woman's Day*, *Metro* newspapers, *Men's Health*, *True Story*, *Seventeen*, *Complete Woman'* magazines, *The New York Times*, and *Oprah Magazine*. She's a monthly dating expert on *JDate's JMag*.

In 2012, after a bout with breast cancer, Dr. Sherman founded Parachute Jump Publishing in order to write a legacy of books to "inspire people to love more." A video about her book legacy was featured in the *Huffington Post* (www.huffingtonpost.com/dr-terri-kennedy/cancer-awareness_b_1967586.html). She has written twenty-five books so far, won eleven book awards and her books are currently translated into German, French, Italian, Spanish, Czech, Korean and Chinese.

Dr. Sherman does life coaching by phone and Skype internationally. She also does psychotherapy in her office in Manhattan.


www.DrPauletteSherman.com

# OTHER BOOKS BY
# DR. PAULETTE KOUFFMAN SHERMAN

## Your Cancer Path (4 Book Set)

- *My Quick Guide Through Breast Cancer: Diagnosis, Surgery, Chemo & Radiation*, Book 1

- *The Cancer Path: A Spiritual Journey into Healing Wholeness & Love*, Book 2

- *My Date with Cancer: 21 Spiritual Lessons*, Book 3

- *The Create Your Own Cancer Path Workbook*, Book 4

## The When Mars Women Date Series (3 Book Set)

- *When Mars Women Date: How Career Women Can Love Themselves Into the Relationship of Their Dreams*, Vol. 1

- *The Mars Women in Relationships Workbook: For the Successful Career Woman Who Wants to Create a Balanced, Romantic Partnership*, Vol. 2

- *We Are From One Planet*, Vol. 3 (a children's book)

# Dating & Relationship Books

- *Dating from the Inside Out: How to Use the Law of Attraction in Matters of the Heart*

- *Facebook Dating: from 1st Date to Soulmate*

- *The Law of Attraction in Marriage*

- *The Law of Atraction in Marriage Action Journal: 77 Practices to Create the Marriage of Your Dreams*

- *A Shared Vision: 100 Conversations to Co-Create the Relationship of Your Dreams*

- *100 Ways to Treat Your Mate like Royalty: Under $10*

- *Dating Advice from Hi to I Do*

- *The Book of Sacred Baths: 52 Bathing Rituals to Revitalize your Life*

- *60+ Inexpensive NYC Dating Ideas*

- *The Lovely Misery of Dating* (fiction)

## Shekhina 3-Part Picture Book Series (illustrated by Rachel Shana Vine)

- *Shekhina*

- *Mishkan*

- *Lift Shekhina Up!*

# Other Books

- *How to Use Your iPad As Your Life Coach*

- *My Bubby's Journey Through the Holocaust*

- *How to Create a Fantastic Fairy Tea Party (With Hardly Any Cooking)*

- *To Be Noble*

You can order these 25 books on Amazon under Paulette Kouffman Sherman. They are part of a legacy of books 'to inspire people to love more' that I began after my recovery from Stage 2 breast cancer.

Dr. Paulette Kouffman Sherman's websites:
www.DrPauletteSherman.com
www.ParachuteJumpPublishing.com

See you soon!
With Love, Light, & Blessings,
Paulette

18647712R00036